FEAR STALKS
THE LAND!

FEAR STALKS THE LAND!

A Commonplace Book

THOM YORKE AND STANLEY DONWOOD

CANONGATE

First published in Great Britain, the USA and Canada in 2021
by Canongate Books Ltd, 14 High Street, Edinburgh EH1 1TE

Distributed in the USA by Publishers Group West
and in Canada by Publishers Group Canada

canongate.co.uk

1

British Library Cataloguing-in-Publication Data
A catalogue record for this book is available on
request from the British Library

ISBN 978 1 83885 736 3

Design © Rafaela Romaya
Typeset in Palatino

Printed and bound in Great Britain by Clays Ltd, Elcograf S.p.A.

to our former selves,
where ever they may be now,
and to all those who knew them

your royal highnesses

      i am citizen insane i am citizen insane i am citizen isane
i am citizen insane i am citizen isnsane i am citizen insane i
i am citizen insane i am citizen insane i am citizen insane i
i am citizen insane i am citizen isnanse i am citizen insane i am
i am citizen insane i am citizen insane i am citiz em insane i am
i am citizen insane i am citizen insane i am citizen insane i am citizen
i am citizen insane i am citizen insane i am citizen insanni am
BODIes floting   walking like   muddy river in bits am piece 3
walking like   graves machine guns in hand.
devils walking in jungles.

CONTENTS

01 WINNING

The last player left in the game is the winner.

02 AIRBORNE

One rainy day whilst out shopping for groceries,
I am surrounded by a growing crowd who are
    under the impression I can fly.

It seems a dreadful mistake has been made:
the local paper has printed an article about a gentle-
    man who really does have this enviable talent,
but they have put my photograph above the article.

I am unsure about how the newspaper came to have
    a picture of me,
but that is the least of my worries,
faced,
as I am,
with this heckling crowd of strangers.

I protest, but the crowd will give no quarter until I
    show them my incredible powers.

At last,
I give in to them,
and stand,
flapping my arms and jumping as high as I can into
    the damp air.

This goes on for some time,
and I become increasingly frightened that the now
    disenchanted crowd will attack me,
believing me to me a self-promoting charlatan.

But in the end they straggle off,
muttering.

Thanking my lucky stars,
I rush home,
too upset to continue my shopping.

That evening,
alone,
I once again try to fly.

It proves to be a futile exercise,
but addictive.

Night after night I stand on my roof,
flapping my arms and making small jumps on
   the tiles.

Try as I might,
I never manage to get airborne.

03 INDEX IN THE WRONG PLACE

A

a dead pyramid of paper
adrift
a spike in his forks
a cane in his spokes
a __ wants this laptop back
animalus
ants
air-conditioning
a grin like road kill
angelus novus (by paul klee)
all I need is a good night's sleep
appallingly close friends
all lickety spit
a million notes at high speed
an amnesiac falling down a hill
an albatross
all I know is that this doesn't feel right
a conflict of interest
according to our survey
american airforce base
all zones
airbrushed
antidotes for loneliness in the goldfish bowl
asbestos (playing with or breaking)
alpha beta gamma zeta
a capsule sent into space
and the lame shall walk
and the blind shall see
and that was last week

B

black rabbit
blue collar
bloated
battery hens
but I couldn't move
birds falling out of the sky
by proxy
blackhole urinal
breaking up
backseat
being poisoned by the staff
bringing in the bailiffs
bent copper

C

care bears falling dead out of the sky
children soon and seals
consumer durables
the captain's head in a bottle
captains of industry
cross the picket line
confusion
conclusions
congratulations!
cockroach
cloud fucking cuckoo land
couldn't take the strain
carpet land

claiming immunity
casualties
clicks on the phone
cling / clinging
chaos on the streets
carbon-coloured
celebrity fund-raising
crew dead

D

days will go from boom to bust
do you see light at the end of the tunnel?
do this before you forget
dead soldiers
deathly hush
duped
dancing to death
drowning in detergent
democracy
dropping like flies
don't feel stupid
doctor, I can't feel my hands

E

eighteen years of cruising
everyone around here
everybody stops and gawps
e.g., genetically-modified bears
easy answers

Spirits and monsters in the forest

end of boom time
even his accent
ethnological footage of lost tribes
educated mediocrats
everything washes over you like a shipwreck

F

forceps
force-fed comparisons
fat cats
farmland is turning to dust
follow the yellow brick road, and so on
flooded house
floating above
frozen to the spot as the flash bulbs erupt

G

geopolitic
ghosts, spooks, spirits and monsters in the forest
grave-robbers
go to bed
goodnight
goddamn you for doing this to us
got to keep your feet on the ground
get with the program
gin palace
glints amongst the ice
genetically guaranteed intelligence

group of seven
going out of town
geek tycoon
genocide

H

heaven
HA HA HA HA HA HA HA HA HA HA Ahhh HA
   HA HA HA AH HA HA AH AH HA HA
humiliation
happy clappy
hyperion
here come the insects with giant teeth and acid blood
helicopter
how I made my millions
hung by the mob
horseflies
house destroyed
how am I driving?
hoping for happy accidents

I

I see no patterns here
in the Hamptons
I decided to move out
is he good to you?
I am scared I might stay like this forever
I am not an expert. I don't know what I am talking
   about

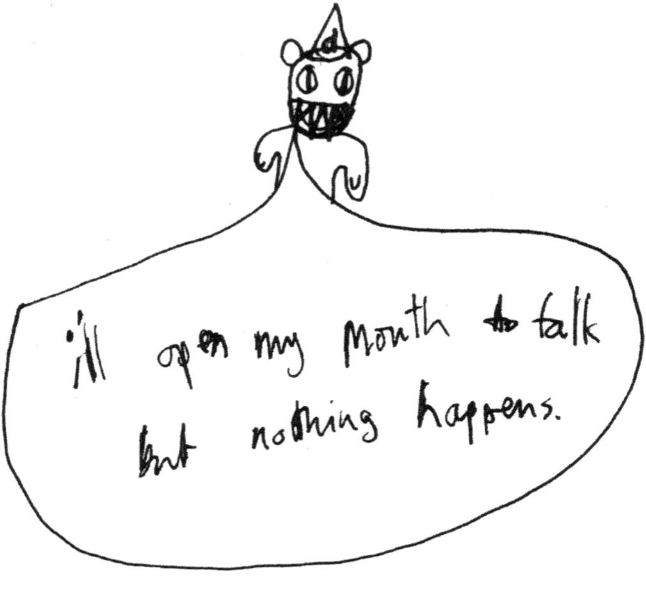
i'll open my mouth to talk
but nothing happens.

I don't understand a word you say and you seem
    so far away
I know when to stop
I am staying at Holiday Inn, room 320
in his will
I think it's too harrowing
I have born a monster, no pulse, stuck on face
I find it difficult to be optimistic
I'm not living in the past. The past is a bastard
it's like only being able to play one song
it'll all blow over soon
I have a paper here that entitles me to fast-track
    status
illuminati
in the face of reality
in the gap in between
invisible forces speaking in a tongue that dribbles
    and lashes
initiation ceremonies
I saw the sky turn green
I love my work
it would be just like me to fuck this up

J

job
just a bumpy ride
just because you can

K

king ludd
king rat
kiss ass
keep the lid on

L

lizard skin
lightning reactions
little birds on the trees all lining up
learn how to swim before the ship sinks
leave it to the experts
look out the window what do you see?
look at him go
like a discontinued component in a
newoutdatedappliance
lost in woods
lynch mob
lame shite excuses
lose some of that fat kids
limitless scenarios
lamps are going out all over Europe

M

my hands are tied; what can I do?
my words are out of ink

middle England
made in China
morning bell
massacre
making life taste better
Murdoch
make over
mass amnesia
mass hysteria
megalomania
meaningless distraction
more mental gossip
moth's cortex crushing thud
mummy and daddy polar bears
mother nature has her own special ways of fighting
    back

    N

nomenklatura
normalcy
the national anthem
nurseryland
no chance of explanation
north birds plead for a habitat from victimization
no defence against the witch-hunt
no blood no mess just reheat
no guilt / no conscience
New York blossoms
new clothes
no rain ever comes

Mass amnesia, mass hysteria

nowadays I get panicked that I have ceased to exist
no sympathy for the victim

O

offerings
oligarchy
optimistic auto-suggestion
opinion polls suggest
occidental
orient
one nine eight
over there, to the east, everything is realistic and
    local and as it should be, except on fire
only window shopping
or your money back

P

paper-tiger
part of the peace process
pig iron
pins & needles
passive inhaler slowing down a bit
predecessor
pork barrels
peace-of-mind
primetime
power games
please remember that past performance is not
    necessarily a guide to future performance

power cut
photo opportunities
please hang up the phone
pilgrim
prepacked newborn slave
people's party
people's princess
people are frightened to leave their homes
pall-bearers

Q

quangos
quick fix

R

rich man in the castle, poor man at the gate
renegade Marxist terrorists
rubber bullets
rather exhausting

S

sarky cogs, skwrking round
system only
starting a family
smokers who have tried everything
saccharine
scrape me off the ceiling
security men

sizzling south west
semen-stained dress
(sample footsteps in all different rooms & textures)
sorry, we were only kidding
shot in the head
silver statue
short sharp shock
soap
short attention span
siren
Sultan of Brunei
successful parents
something to lean on
strangers in the camp
sinking sand
share options
shopping in the real world
skwirm
spin with a grin
swarms
stateless
successor generation network
salivates in the ashes
stolen
sick of rushing
silhouettes dashing
strangled beaten up
slave
scarecrows made of straw
someone must be to blame
snow alert

Learn how to swim before the ship sinks

shiny polished floors
shiny medals
stuck in the mud
straw dogs to scare the crows
stuck on a pin
super being
stampede starts

T

torrid Tuesday
they're dropping everywhere
take my advice
take the highs with the lows
technicolor
telephone company
there are loads of school kids hanging round
the empire will grow and grow
to look a dead man in the eye
trickle down
the toys all kill the grown-ups
to educate small children in weighty matters such as
    organised religon
today I just ran out of excuses
talking to the people next door
this shouldn't happen
top floor is unsafe
three men in a bed
tourists pissed off at having their holidays interrupted
    by revolution
threats have decimated homes to sludge

think nice thoughts
the bloody power of kings
there is so much traffic
the Labour Party claims it was their idea
the cameras will not save you now . . . or then
thumb invitation
this is a wake-up call
turning bear civilisations to warming and floating

U

unconditional surrender
upon receipt of the monies
unhinged
unsatisfactory
unless of course you're trying to hide something?

V

ventriloquists

W

welfare state
where are you?
we shall all be bled to death
with a grin like road kill
what it's like to be shot
what have I done wrong?
when they talk about you like you're not there
weapons of mass destruction

well-adjusted
who are you kidding?
woods where no birds sing
what's in the briefcase?
we fix your dollars
watch the world collapse
worry
wood of suicides
windfall
what's so wrong with that?
winter palace
when you wish upon a star
when they talk about you as if you can't hear
when the diggers return
who are the hip one hundred?
we'll see who was right and who was wrong

X

x ray ok

Y

you shouldn't worry; worry is a killer
you're so hostile
you're just bluffing
you have such an aura dahling
you were the one
you will soon be on the scrapheap in bits and pieces
you crossed the line
your moon is out of orbit

your lips are cold
your eyes are beach stones
yellow eyes
your tide has turned but won't turn back
your home is at risk if you do not keep up
    repayments
you're safe until you look away
you don't know what you're talking about

you are no expert
your choice
you poor thing

I am scared I might stay like this for ever

04 PULK/PULL REVOLVING DOORS

there are barn doors

and there are revolving doors

and doors with many windows

there are doors in doors

and doors on beds

doors in the rudders of big ships

and there are trapdoors

there are doors that open by themselves

there are sliding doors and secret doors

there are doors that lock and doors that don't

there are doors that let you in and out but never open

and there are trapdoors

that you can't come back from.

05 ICE AGE AND SO ON

glaciers
the ice age
the end of everything
a blank empty battlefield
everyone's gone home
there's nothing to see here
go away
blood-filled swimming pools
death
freezing agony
nostalgia
the past idealised
there is no future
noises of crunching metal
torn ligaments
cover-ups
spilt blood
split oil
have a look
roll up roll up

ok
I'm

I can't continue[1]

---

1 **Addendum**
  Selected examples of ice melt around the world, circa 1999

ARCTIC SEA ICE
Arctic Ocean
Has shrunk by 6% since 1978, with a 14% loss of thicker,

year-round ice. Has thinned by 40% in less than 30 years.

GREENLAND ICE SHEET
Greenland
Has thinned by more than a metre a year on its southern and eastern edges since 1993.

COLUMBIA GLACIER
Alaska, United States
Has retreated nearly 13 kilometres since 1982. In 1999, retreat rate increased from 25 metres per day to 35 metres per day.

GLACIER NATIONAL PARK
Rocky Mountains, United States
Since 1850, the number of glaciers has dropped from 150 to fewer than 50. Remaining glaciers could disappear completely in 30 years.

ANTARCTIC SEA ICE
Southern Ocean
Ice to the west of the Antarctic Peninsula decreased by some 20% between 1973 and 1993, and continues to decline.

PINE ISLAND GLACIER
West Antarctica
Grounding line (where glacier hits ocean and floats) retreated 1.2 kilometres a year between 1992 and 1996. Ice thinned at a rate of 3.5 metres per year.

LARSEN B ICE SHELF
Antarctic Peninsula
Calved a 200 kilometre² iceberg in early 1998. Lost an additional 1,714 kilometre² during the 1998–1999 season, and 300 kilometre² so far during the 1999–2000 season.

TASMAN GLACIER
New Zealand
Terminus has retreated 3 kilometres since 1971, and main front has retreated 1.5 kilometres since 1982. Has thinned by up to 200 metres on average since the 1971–82 period. Icebergs began to break off in 1991, accelerating the collapse.

MEREN, CARSTENZ AND NORTHWALL FIRN GLACIERS
Irian Jaya, Indonesia
Rate of retreat increased to 45 metres a year in 1995, up from only 30 metres a year in 1936. Glacial area shrank by some

84% between 1936 and 1995.
Meren Glacier is now close to disappearing altogether.

DOKRIANI BAMAK GLACIER
Himalayas, India
Retreated by 20 metres in 1998, compared with an average
    retreat of 16.5 metres over the previous 5 years. Has
    retreated a total of 805 metres since 1990.

DUOSUOGANG PEAK
Ulan Ula Mountains., China
Glaciers have shrunk by some 60% since the early 1970s.

TIAN SHAN MOUNTAINS
Central Asia
Twenty-two per cent of glacial ice volume has disappeared in
    the past 40 years.

CAUCASUS MOUNTAINS
Russia
Glacial volume has declined by 50% in the past century.

ALPS
Western Europe
Glacial area has shrunk by 35 to 40% and volume has declined
    by more than 50% since 1850. Glaciers could be reduced to
    only a small fraction of their present mass within decades.

MOUNT KENYA
Kenya
Largest glacier has lost 92% of its mass since the late 1800s.

*~ limitless
scenarios,
limitless
channels*

SPEKA GLACIER
Uganda
Retreated by more than 150 metres between 1977 and 1990,
    compared with only 35–45 metres between 1958 and 1977.

UPSALA GLACIER
Argentina
Has retreated 60 metres a year on average over the last 60
    years, and rate is accelerating.

QUELCCAYA GLACIER
Andes, Peru
Rate of retreat increased to 30 metres a year in the 1990s, up
   from only 3 metres a year between the 1970s and 1990.

*~ the martians
have landed*

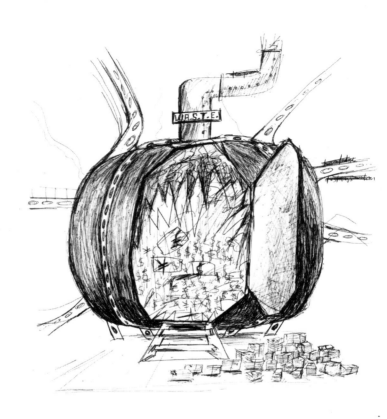

I wait at the edge for the tide to come in
all it brings is empty plastic containers
and sticks and polyethylene

06 LISTEN TO THE RADIO

We listen to the radio sometimes and the politicians
and the generals all seem to be okay.

They can't commit and often they can't comment
either, but we are hiding in the woods and often
have to do both.

When the war is over and all the fires have gone
out we will watch the news.

Then the politicians will be more precise.

Yesterday some people were found in a burnt
house and we knew who the dead were by their
charred clothes. It was hard, otherwise, to tell
who had been who.

WITNESS HAS **EYES** & **MOUTH** SEWN SHUT AT **NIGHT**.

07 GREY GHOSTS

The room is just a room
But blurred grey
Ghosts come in through the door
Blurred shapes with fingers
He is in bed asleep
We see him
In bed
They sew up his eyes one at a time

Then it is morning and the blurred grey ghosts leave
The sun is at the windows
His hands move
He just says 'I can see you'

That's the end.[2]

~ HA HA HA
HA HA HA HA
HA HA HA HA
HA HA HA

~ Please hang
up the phone

---

2 In Manhattan or somewhere

Except all the skyscrapers and buildings are massive bulky hedges
Banks are privet
Insurance offices are laurel
Corporations are beech
Some of the areas are trimmed less frequently and are overrun
    with bindweed
Some conceal barbed wire behind elegantly clipped foliage
You'd think it would be a haven for birds but if it is they don't sing
And at night it's very very still and very very dark
Long shadows from the hedges form in the moonlight

the morning bell
the morning bell
light another candle and
release me, release me

you can keep the furniture
a bump on the head
howling down the chimney
release me, release me

where d'you park the car?
where d'you park the car?
your clothes are on the lawn
with the furniture
now I might as well
I might as well

sleepy jack
the fire drill
round and round and round and round
and round

cut the kids in half
cut the kids in half
cut the kids in half

I wanted to tell you but you never listened

I wanted to tell you but you never listened
I keep walking walking walking walking
lights are on nobody's home everyone wants to be you
lights are on nobody's home everyone wants to be you
I keep walking walking walking walking

yeah

09 LIQUIDISER

I am in a liquidiser.

My head is down the toilet.

Teeth coming out of sockets.

Crawling on hands and knees,

chucked up all my insides on the nice new cream carpet.

Clearly,

you are not impressed.[3]

---

3 We have arrived home

we have arrived home on a jet plane
I am sleeping on the floor in the dust

we pull up near the house
I pull my bags down the middle of the street

a messed-up thin lady in a blue dress, twice my height, is asking
    me for a language
I don't know what she means
in the half light she follows me

I say goodbye to the others as a man hoovers the dust I've been
    sleeping in

There's a party going on in my house
There are spiders in the food

10 KNIVES OUT

I want you to know
he's not coming back
look into my eyes
I'm not coming back

so knives out
catch da mouse
don't look down
shove it in your mouth

if you'd been a dog
they would a drowned you at birth
look into my eyes
it's the only way you'll know I'm telling the truth

so knives out
cook him up
squash his head
put him in the pot

~ you have such
an aura dahling
I want you to know
he's not coming back
he's bloated and frozen
still there's no point in letting it go to waste

~ like a
discontinued
component in a
newly outdated
appliance
so knives out
catch da mouse
squash his head
put him in the pot

11 I CALLED BUT YOU WERE OUT

the people in these songs should have names

guinea pigs
a cheap publicity stunt

the rollercoaster ride of pointlessness
why should you ever wanna get off?

my face is a weather chart and the weather is
    coming fast

hidden in the forest,
lost in the woods,
lost in all directions,
language robbed

THESIS
ANTITHESIS
SYNTHESIS
PARALYSIS

a dead pyramid of paper
mummy and daddy polar bear

to be happy is simple
why create these obstacles for yourself?
imagine yourself befriending an insect

Forget why you went there when you get there

we are all gorgeous
welcome to the party that never stops

it's showtime
playstation

'the majority of the West must accept an end to their
    luxurious lifestyle'
alligators in New York sewers
bacteria in everything

for 'flexibility of labour markets' read 'not
    knowing whether you have a job tomorrow'
£3.20 an hour
it'll all blow over
just a storm in a teacup
powerless state

according to survey / opinion polls suggest
unrest
the ultimate weapon
industrial action

please allow us the suspension of your disbeliefs

more people than ever are now engaged in a
    desperate search for true love
3,089,240 women realised they were trapped in
    loveless relationships; 3,002,783 men

the question is: will they escape?[4]

---

4 A Leviathan

We are being followed
by a dragon in the night
This dragon is a sea dragon
A Leviathan
Every house we go to
is struck by lightning
Lightning keeps striking
wherever we are
The dragon is offering a solution
Any wish is his command
Slowly I realise
the price for this release is my soul;
by this time it is too late

The mist rolls off the sea and surrounds the house.

According to our survey, opinion polls suggest

12 SURVEY

Q1

All participation is a myth.

Q2

I have been manipulated and permanently distorted.

Q10

When you put a gun to my head you aren't fooling anyone.

Q15

Nothing is as I planned it.

Q21

My drug of choice is self-pity.

Q27

After the millenium I will shoot to kill.

Q29

Scientists know what they are talking about.

Q31

It is not in my power to change anything.

Q35

I think the environment will be okay.

Q44

We are lining up to see you fall flat on your face.

Q51

Ultimately, the Millennium Dome is a spectacular monument to the doublethink of our times.

Q53

Looking into my eyes is the only way you'll know I'm telling the truth.

Q55

If I won the lottery I would keep all the money and wallpaper my house with it.

Q56

In this bunker there are women and children. There are no weapons.

Q59

I am no longer prepared to give you the benefit of the doubt.

Q68

No one appears to be able to help me.

Q72

I hate myself but have no clear idea why.

Q75

I figure one day I will get unlucky.

Q76

The lyrics in pop songs seem to describe my life uncannily accurately.

Q96

I start many things but have yet to finish a single one.

Q101

I am getting worse rather than better.

Q108

The innocent have nothing to hide.

Q110

I'm working on a novel, actually.

Q117

Mobile telephones make people look important and busy.

Q133

I am fed up with being taken for a ride.

Q134

Genetically-engineered children will be a reality in my lifetime.

Q135

I always set my watch fast so I am never late.

Q136

No amount of careful precaution can save me from random chaotic violence.

Q144

I am fucking sick of being patronised by television.

Q149

Celebrities have blurry unfinished eyes.

Q150

I hope that no tax-payers money is going towards this.[5]

---

5 Click Here

The camera's clever disguise allows it to be set up on a shelf almost anywhere & immediately blend in with surrounding fixtures.

Optional accessories allow unattended, self-contained recording for days.

Features built-in low light, B & W video camera

380 TV lines resolution for crisp, detailed video

12VDC operation for use with internal batteries or AC adapter

Standard RCA connections for use with external recorder

Price: $599.95

13 LIKE SPINNING PLATES

the bodies floating downstream
the truck-loads with machetes
the cameras are turning off
avert your gaze

the birds pick over the bodies
the cameras & the flies
the dead can come back to life
cut your tails with a carving knife

bloated just like rotten trees
eyes popped out
flashing across the 9 o'clock news

the make-up will run
the set will roll away

you will soon be on the scrapheap
the cameras will not save you now or then

bodies floating down the muddy river

like rotten wood
eyes popped out like cigarette machines
the cameras will be gone
the make-up will run
the set will roll away

we shall all be bled to death to feed cloud
    cuckoo land

they're killing all the tall thin ones
we will all be cut to shreds
I am citizen insane
spontaneous combustion
all history is frozen
all I do is spin these plates
you're too bloody beautiful by far
baby in a bubble
it'll all blow over soon
why me?
having not said goodbye? having not made amends

~ I think it's too harrowing, all I need is a good night's sleep
sit tight and wait for it to go away
a kid stuck in a bottle
a cane in his spokes
the cameras do nothing to save you
to watch you chopped to pieces by machetes
I watched you on TV

~ all lickety spit
bodies floating down the muddy river
we killed all the tall thin ones

~ an amnesiac falling down a hill

~ a conflict of interest, a poisoned guilty conscience, days will from boom to bust
while you make pretty speeches I'm being cut to shreds

you feed me to the lions. a delicate balance

when this just feels like spinning plates

~ doctor I can't feel my hands
I'm living in cloud cuckoo land

~ everybody stops and gawps
and this just feels like spinning plates
our bodies floating down the muddy river

[52]

I saw the sky turn green

14 EXCLAMATION MARKS

Some of the days that go by should have
   exclamation marks after them.
Yesterday had photorealistic houses but painted
   flames coming from the roofs.
I saw it from up on the hill when I was looking
   for food!

15 FOLLOW ME AROUND

you follow me around
an echo down the slipway
a falling satellite
the moon upon the shadows
the way the water pulls you in
your twisted vengeance

I always seem to miss
I need to see a shrink

I skirt around artistically
in 1990s irony
prodding
spitting
will not let it be

the smashed fragments
river into sea

you're not asleep and this is not a dream

death and the maiden
the figure that fucks you when you're asleep

on your back
his demon shape shadow over you

you cannot move
you cannot yell out

once you've seen him he never leaves your side
is with you always

this is the night hag

send me to the asylum

you used to be like us
now you're one of them
you are turning into one of them

'but I would like to change back now please'
sorry
it's too late

disco inferno

I see you in the dark
Corner of the street
Coming after me

Headlights on full beam
Coming down the fast lane
Coming after me

You follow me around
You follow me around

Blowing holes in everything
Thatcher's children
See you on the way back down

You follow me around
You follow me around

Nowadays I get panicked
I cease to exist
I have ceased to exist

I feel absolutely nothing
The words are out of ink
The words, you know, are out of ink

They follow me around
They follow me around

I would like to change back now
To the shadow of
The shadow of my former self

It follows me around
It follows me around

Did you lie to us?
We thought you were different
Now you know we're not so sure

Drooling looney tunes
Moving in a swarm
Moving in a swarm

*~ I have been
manipulated and
permanently
distorted, I have
born a monster,
no pulse and
stuck on face, its
guts wrenched
out and chewed*

16 PACKT LIKE SARDINES
IN A CRUSHD TIN BOX

after years of waiting, nothing came.

**as your life flashed before your eyes
you realise
you were looking in the wrong place.**

I'm a reasonable man

get off my case[6]

*~ hymns on
a blackboard,
shiny polished
floors*

---

6 packt like sardines in a crushd tin box

always looking in the wrong place
small children in a sandpit

playing in the sun

grandmas and happy couples

all of this could have been yours

if you'd not been such a jerk

if you'd not been such an idiot

after years of waiting
nothing came

as your life flashed before your eyes
you realise

you were looking in the wrong place

I'm a reasonable man

get off my case

17 CUTTOOTH

I would live a wallpaper life
or run away to the Foreign Legion
I would live a wallpaper life
or run away to the Foreign Legion

as the tanks roll into town
as the tanks roll into town
a little bit of knowledge will destroy you
a little bit of knowledge will destroy you

I don't know why I feel so tongue-tied
don't know why I feel so skinned alive

run until your lungs are sore
until you cannot feel it any more
run until your lungs are sore
until you find that open door
build you up to pull you down
tie me to my feet and watch me drown.
build you up to pull you down
tie you to the stake and watch in you burn in hell!

I don't know why I feel so tongue-tied
don't know why I feel so skinned alive

I'll find another skin to wear
I'll find another skin to wear

~ A giant
wind machine
(several)

18 SCHEDULE

Plan C
Amendment 7

Here's the schedule

C will pick you up at 8.30 a.m.
In a shiny car

You will then proceed to the hotel

Whereupon
At 10.30 a.m.
You will meet X, the press officer
To run through any questions you may have

At 11.30 a.m.
The film crew is booked for the interview in a room
somewhere in the hotel
The interviewer's name is N. (pronounced 'N')

The questions:

1. What does your recent promotion mean to you?

2. Briefcases; which are most important to you?
What are you most concerned / angry about? e.g.
imitation leather, brass corners, uncomfortable
handles etc.

3. Does the business community have a special
responsibility to speak out on behalf of these issues?

4. How do you think global economic meltdown will change attitudes?

5. Bunkers; how do you expect the public will respond when they discover that there are corporate bunkers complete with anti-personnel weapons under the city?

6. Your own impressions; this was a little vague and they were open to direction from you but it was something along the lines of you having freedom of movement within the Canary Wharf development.

This is pre-recorded so you have control.
You can cut anything you are not comfortable with.

~ 18 years of cruising

~ invisible forces speaking in a tongue that dribbles and lashes, salivates in the ashes, in the gap in between you and me

Everyone
Everyone around here
Everyone is so
near
is holding on

is holding on

Everyone
Everyone is so near
Everyone has got the fear
is holding on

is holding on

FRIGHTFULLY BAD FOR BUSINESS.

MODIFIED BEAR:
ZEMPOALA,
MEXICO.

20 ADVICE FOR ROBOTS

If feel that low again
Please try remain
inside circle of friends

Softness
Shaking
All in its right being

It will pass
Only part
Not the last

Salt water good
For cleaning

Snapshots
Sentient beings
cold (soothing)

Don't

Go

Will only want to come back

Not a circle
Not just being
(our radiance)
(our meaning)

Sorry that didn't. Write (be there)
When you wanted. Write (be there)

Now writing
Now saying

Please remember
All the good things

red wine and sleeping pills
help me get back to your arms
cheap sex and sad films
help me get where I belong

I think you're crazy maybe
I think you're crazy maybe

stop sending letters
letters always get burnt
its not like the movies
they fed us on little white lies

beautiful angel
pulled apart at birth
limbless and helpless
I can't even recognise you

I think you're crazy maybe
I think you're crazy maybe

I will see you
in the next life

22 FUCKER

Paper bag advice (to be stamped on the side of all
   paper bags)

side A.
Blow into this paper bag
go home
and stop grinning at everyone.

side B.
If the boss sits there and accuses you of stealing,
of not having the right motivation,
don't just sit there and take it,
hit the fucker in the face.

23 FAX CORRESPONDENCE (example)

All the meetings are going to plan; we've been in
  contact with X and he is willing to wear our
  lipstick on condition that we don't reveal his
  days of 'pot-smoking' with Y.
We told the heavies to pull out and go visit Z.

N was a dead loss but he showed a slight interest in
  our eye-shadow. He uses it now when he makes
  his speeches.

Also plague in H has meant we will have to stop
  live experiments. Apparently it is difficult to
  establish a control for the experiment.

As always all information is highly confidential.

PS
I included some useful slogans I thought up to sell
  our new range. Please tick the ones you like.

24 YOU AND WHOSE ARMY?

you think it's so easy
come on come on
you and whose army?
I have God on my side and am not afraid to die
I know there's a place in heaven for me
barbecue on CNN
arms bazaar on CNN
all over in the flick of a switch
let's see what you've won
come on centurians
ripples in a pond
tomahawks
apologies and condolences
security forces

itchy fingers on triggers
mothers gone to the butchers
in the bunker like sitting ducks
you and whose army?
(cut your nose to spite your face)

come on come on
you think you'll drive us crazy
well
come on come on

you and whose army?
you and your cronies?

come on come on

~ they'll
trample you
underfoot as
they stampede,
as they run
screaming and
wailing with
sad panic in
their eyes

Holy Roman Empire
come on if you think
come on if you think
you can take us on
you can take us on

you and whose army?
you and your cronies?
you forget so easy . . .

we ride tonight
we ride tonight
ghost horses
ghost horses
we ride tonight
we ride tonight
ghost horses
ghost horses
ghost horses

25 HOW VERY TWISTED

How very responsible
How very generous
How very kind of you
How very genteel
How very glamorous
How very comfortable
Just what I asked for

How very clever
How very reasonable
How very thought out
How very practical
How very useful
How very generous

~ celebrity
fundraising

What a clever use of words[7]

---

7 **People of Today 2000**

Reverend Peter Peter
Lord and Lady Doherty
Professor Byron Bryon Byron
Viscount Down of Yorkshire
Alan Lee, Peter, Writer, Times, Racing, Tennis etc.
Reginald Anthony Hungerford Lechmere, guidance (remedial)
    sex-councillor
Professor Siebert Saloman Poyser, (legal) advisor
Timothy Pratt, Esquire
Air Marshall Sir Peter Kinloss
Lady Beatrice Mary, Sheriff, Peer [sic]
Oliphant Oliphant fin attaché, British Embassy. Recreations
    opera, wine
Runcie, Baron.

26 AN ADULT

Adults can say no

Adults have learnt to accept they cannot have everything

Adults eat junk mail

Mail order adults

Adults avoid traffic congestion

Adults, in black because it suits them

An adult will wear a gorilla costume to join in

An adult, in times of loneliness, will try anything

Adults strap ballast to themselves to weigh them down

Or become lost souls wandering

An adult loses interest in all things so keeps lists

Like this one

Adults cannot make up their minds

An adult feels like they've lost something

27 ALWAYS ASK

be one to guarantee
capitalist pick
get corporate cosmocrat
system only American-educated mediocrats
eighteen years of cruising
rather exhausting
air conditioning
thumb invitation
conclusions
even his accent
Prague, Manhattan
force-fed comparisons
silhouettes dashing
I think it is too harrowing
in the Hamptons
economy venture capitalism
floating above
successful parents
going out of town
property conversations

~ upon receipt of the monies it's like only being able to play one song
talking to the people next door
New York blossoms
especially counterpoint

~ same shit different label genetically guaranteed intelligence
venture kindergarten
appallingly close friends
share options
I couldn't understand a word he said
you poor thing
when you leave spare a thought for

ten minutes but do not be late
dot com
expecting
now master humanised
collect the prize
maggots and worms
other guests
sophisticated friends
always ask[8]

---

8 our little bit of England

to be eaten and regurgitated
repackaged in prissy little boxes
marketed till we really believe we want it more than life itself
till we don't know any different
stone cold dead on our being dragged around by our nostrils
cameras flashing at blinking natives
we appreciate the culture
as we call in the butchers with the hamburgers
queueing up to see the freaks
our little bit of England

28 LIFE IN A GLASSHOUSE

don't throw stones and don't talk politics
your royal highnesses
don't throw stones and don't get in a tizz
your royal highnesses

CCTV in every room
zooming lenses in the trees
they are going through your shit
rummaging through the rubbish for something they
    can sell to the newspapers

you are a depressive
you are being optimistic
you are being very negative

the quiet blue gas flames gently
hissing fingers round my heart
who is going to forgive me?
living in a glasshouse

I'm a white mouse, pink nose, pink eyes
hungry for food trapped in a cage
living in a glasshouse

in the eye of the tornado
nosey parkers
sniffing round
snide remarks
living in a glasshouse

everybody wants a piece of window pane
everybody wants a piece of broken glass
everybody wants a shattered piece of the windows
to show their friends
to take it home with them
and watch the light turning into rainbows.

I am sick of fucking mind games
I am sick of getting blamed

unforgiving and pencil sharp
well at least you look the part
think nice thoughts
living in a glasshouse

~ your home is
at risk

once again I'm in trouble with my only friend,
she is papering the window panes,
she is putting on a smile,
living in a glasshouse

once again pack'd like frozen food and battery
    hens
think of all the starving millions
don't talk politics and don't throw stones,
your royal highnesses

well of course I'd like to sit to around and chat
well of course I'd like to stay and chew the fat
well of course I'd like to sit around and chat
but someone's listening in

once again we are hungry for a lynching
that's a strange mistake to make
you should turn the other cheek
living in a glasshouse

well of course I'd like to sit around and chat
well of course I'd like to stay and chew the fat
well of course I'd like to sit around and chat only
    only only
only only only
only only only
only only only
there's someone listening in[9]

---

9 Hunting Bears

3.15 a.m.
up ahead
I see
something
on 42nd street
middle of the deserted road

as we come close
I hear
a woman screaming and crying
a few passers-by have stopped to look
blood
pouring
as if from a tap

we slow as we pass
as the blood pumps out

we drive on in silence
listening to the woman's scream
dying away in the distance

My everyday life.

Thick smoke, no breeze.

And how do you see yourself in fifty years' time?

Place for credits of movie about missing persons.

We plants are happy plants.

200 people faint. Hard to breathe.

Roll up roll up see my collection of small things on ~~ the chance of a lifetime?~~ *roll up roll up*

better ↓

The more you drive, the less intelligent you get.

Hit the road quick.

Oxygen should be regarded as a drug.

Thick smoke not evenly distributed. Visibility 50m.

If you don't ask me out to dinner I don't eat.

Lobster-skin-shopping-mall-coffee-stained-lipsync.

A wardrobe painted in fairground colours.

Story begins with explosion. Ends with explosion.

Your fantasies are unlikely. But beautiful.

No substitute for a healthy smile.

It occurs to him that if he died that night,

He would have died happy. Because he was loved.

Has sex ever really moved you to a different place?

Reduced enjoyment and pleasure.

The smoke came back extremely thick and abrasive.

People are aware, but not that bothered.

Heavy artillery concealed in nose.

Everything I do/say is suspect.

A stranglers' hands.

One of us.

No autonomy. A lethal coctail. Horrific violence.

29 EVERYTHING IN ITS RIGHT PLACE

yes

I am not hearing straight
I cannot be hearing straight
I must be completely stone deaf

you see yesterday I wasn't hearing straight
but today everything is in its right place

~ (the captain's
head in a bottle) he was a good man they said,
he was a gentleman they said

even when life spat in his face
he put everything back
in its right place

nothing but blue skies from now on
no ghosts
no skeletons

I keep thinking
I will wake up tomorrow and
it will all be
gone

everything_____

**in its right place in its right place in its right place
        in its right place**

yesterday I woke up   sucking a
      lemon   yesterday I

woke   up sucking
    a lemon   yesterday

I   woke   up
  sucking a
             lemon   yesterday I
   woke   up
   sucking

   a   lemon _____
   everything_____

in its right place right place right place right place

                   there are
                   two colours
                   in my
                   head

          there are
          two colours
          in my head what

what was that you
tried to say?
what
      what was that you tried to say
                   tried

to

say

tried

to   say

tried to

say

tried   to say

~ (I see no   tried to   say_____
patterns
here)   _____

[84]

30 PITCH THIS

How do these grab you?

Pitch One: Escaping from a burning hotel. No shoes.
It's raining. Do you go back into the burning hotel
and find shoes, or get your feet wet?

Pitch Two: Wander into a school room by mistake. All
the children know your name and your darkest
secrets. Do you run? Or make the best of it?

Pitch Three: Answering a phone in a call box on top
of a hill. It's the Devil. Do you slam the phone
down or attempt conversation?[10]

---

10 My week
with Stanley Donwood

Sunday
Nothing much

Monday
Woke up
Wandered around the house

Tuesday
Went to the shops

Wednesday
Watched Kilroy

Thursday
Phone the All-Bran advice line

Friday
Nothing much

Saturday
Pulled legs off a spider

Next week: Saddam Hussein

31 BURNT-OUT TANK

some people get lucky

some people don't

there's a lot of unlucky people at the moment

what the papers tell you is all true

the lives of the rich and famous are more fulfilled

pin the tail on the donkey

on a burnt-out tank

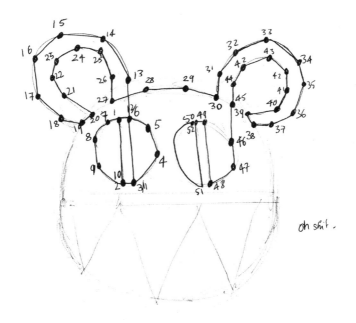

oh shit.

edited fucked up
strangled beaten up

32 I MIGHT BE WRONG

I might be wrong
I might be wrong
I could have sworn I saw a light
coming on

I used to think
I used to think
there was no future left at all
I used to think

open up
begin again

let's go down the waterfall
think about the the good things
and never look back
and never look back
and never look back

what would I do?
what would I do?
if I did not have you?

open and up and let me in

That there
That's not me
I go
where I please
I walk through walls
I float down the Liffey

I'm not here
This isn't happening
I'm not here
~ you poor   I'm not here
thing

In a little while
~ other guests   I'll be gone
~ do this before   The moment's already passed
you forget   Yeah it's gone

And I'm not here
This isn't happening
I'm not here
~ elephant steps   I'm not here

Strobe lights
And blowing speakers
Fireworks
~ there's not   And hurricanes
a day goes by
that I am not
grateful for   I'm not here
what I am   This isn't happening
I'm not here
~ click your   I'm not here
heels twice,
wish yourself
anywhere   [90]

It'll all blow over soon

34 FOG

There's a little child running round this house
And he never leaves
He will never leave

And the fog comes up from the sewers
And glows in the dark

Baby alligators in the sewers
Grow up fast
Anything you want, it can be done

How?

How did you go bad?

Did you go bad?

35 HOLIDAY INN, ROOM 320

what's in the briefcase?

I have a paper here that entitles me to fast track status

I have fast-track status
why don't anyone stop, anyone stop to let me out?

everybody stops and gawps
and lines the motorway
throwing flowers at the hearse

you crossed the line

Holiday Inn room 320

I sing the revolution
you tuck into the bloody steak

sink the pound sink the euro
we'll fix your dollars and cents
string them up
they dance like puppets
dancing to our tune

let's see what we've won   *~ adrift*

limitless scenarios
limitless channels
on which to watch

we'll watch the flames
and the valleys
we'll watch the boots and the blood
we'll see who was right
and who was wrong

the dead can come back to life
cut your tails with a carving knife

this year's monsters
this year only
no news is good news

don't jeopardise your position

and we are faceless
you can't attack us
we're ascending
you cannot follow us
we are wondrous
you will bow to us

*~ e.g. genetically
modified bears*   I have born a monster
no pulse
a stuck-on face
in the woods, where no birds sing

sing me a lullaby
I'm tired
and I wanna get to sleep tonight

36 BOMB ON THE PLANE

people
with novels
comforting screaming babies
staring straight ahead

in the panic
the stewardess is desperate
she is shouting
at those standing
those who demand their extra inches of space
first in the queue

packed
sardines
with a bomb

the babies maintain their crying vigil

the upper class take comfort in their space
their upgrade
in the event of anything untoward
they will proceed toward the nearest exit
in a dignified fashion

neatly designed hand luggage
they hold their bags up and inch forward

holiday makers at the end of the trip
with duty free
remember their experiences as best they can

make peace with the world
before taking your seat
on this last flight out of New York this evening
there is a bomb on the plane

children and families first please
excuse me
have I got the window seat I asked for?

37 IDIOTEQUE

Who's in the bunker?
Who's in the bunker?
Women and children first
And the children first
And the children

I'll laugh until my head comes off
I'll swallow till I burst
Until I burst
Until I

*~ all over at
the flick of
a switch*

Who's in the bunker?
Who's in the bunker?
I have seen too much
you haven't seen enough
You haven't seen

I laugh until my head comes off
Women and children first
And children first
And children first
and children

*~ mummy
and daddy
polar bears*

Here I'm alive
Everything all of the time
Here I'm alive
Everything all of the time

Ice age coming
Ice age coming
Let me hear both sides

Let me hear both sides
Let me hear both

Ice age coming
Ice age coming
Throw him in the fire
Throw him in the fire
Throw him in the

We're not scaremongering
This is really happening
~ hung by the   Happening
mob

We're not scaremongering
This is really happening
Happening

~ crew dead   Mobiles skwrking
Mobiles chirping
Take the money run
Take the money run
~ let's see what   Take the money
you've won

Here I'm alive
Everything all of the time
Here I'm alive
Everything all of the time

Here I'm alive
Everything all of the time
Here I'm alive
~ optimistic   Everything all of the time
auto-suggestion

[98]

he'll take the money from under your nose
use it in his business-friendly world
he'll tell you all want to hear

he paints himself reflective white
to reflect the blast when it comes
he will take your children
and he'll break your homes

he will tell you how hard he is trying
but we're all in the market now
it is a harsh and cruel world

(~ shotgun under the counter)

he says he wants to be our friend
he says he's always been on our side
he's a just a leader with difficult decisions
that you really wouldn't understand
he holds his hands to show his concern
and we believe him

~ a grin like road kill

and the ghosts of the innocent
they are coming back to haunt us
and the blood of the disappeard
who are trapped in the bunkers
you will not hear their screams
from the camera on the end of the missile

38 GOLDEN HANDSHAKE

this is your golden handshake
this is an hallucination
and these faces are in a dream
a computer-generated environment
a fantasy island
you
can
do
anything

and not have to face the consequences

this is your golden handshake
you can put us in freeze frame
you can touch whoever you want
you can move them around into compromising
    positions
strip them naked
screw whoever
or whatever
(although technically they will be frozen to the touch)

sit back down again
and press play
like
nothing
has
happened

That is pure fantasy.

I will be sad to see the snowmen go

There's just the muffled crunchy sound of teeth
grinding and scraping of boots on tarmac or
something and a noise far away that maybe is
someone crying or a cat and everything moves
a bit in the wind

There's a tape on of people talking about nothing
important at a restaurant and a marching sound
that's a bit like a lot of soldiers and a bit like a
wheel rubbing against metal but it might not be
a tape it's hard to tell

And everyone's run out of jokes because no one's
laughing at anything although they probably
would if they had a sense of humour

Probably nothing important

Just a noise in the dark when you're half asleep
something behind the curtains don't look it's
nothing don't look honestly it's nothing

Maybe it's the town you live in making these noises

Maybe it's you

Just a million mobiles and modems squawking and
spluttering and hissing like piss on a fire like a
million gallons of piss on an inferno just think
of that eh?

Just think of that

Vertebrae being sawn apart sounds like this[11]

---

11 **raw fish**

deep fried mars bar
confit of monkey brains
pot noodle
turkey burger
southern style finger food
I dine on only the premium brands

waterfalls of meltwater
gentle needles you can hardly feel

these woods and hills are the trademark of woods and hills plc
    countryside developments

glaciated autoinferno

lovingly scraping the bottom of the oil barrel

eventually I watch war atrocities and the soundtrack makes it okay.

oh very funny.

soandso would like you to call left a message saying
no sound. except you. no sound. except you.
no sound. except you. no sound. except you.

a lot of background noise and a lot of repetition. and we wish
    it was just noise just a trapped bird in the chimney just a
    blockage in a pipe just the boiler just the floorboards just the
    house, settling

try a new lipstick a new colour a new you [this week only]

sorry we were only kidding

bored archangels in the paranoid courts of the gods

And when I opened the curtains they were taking
    the set away and packing up for
the day, the cameras and the lights turned off

The darkness replaced with strip lights and the
    grey skies the blind whirring of machinery

I'd like to write a beautiful story about love[12]

---

12 [copy/paste]

Everyone expects you to perform but you can't
Copy / paste but nothing happens
Undo but can't undo
Get text ha ha ha
I'm a very busy person I'm sorry you'll have to wait until
    tomorrow
or maybe the next day if you're lucky
if I'm lucky
if I'm lucky I'll still be here:
hello how are you is everything okay?
I hope [insert situation] has been satisfactorily resolved ha ha ha

Try t ngage n mnngfl cnvrstn. Try.
ha, ha.

When they talk about you like you're not there
when they talk about you as if you can't hear

40 OPTIMISTIC (OR THE POWER
OF POSITIVE THINKING)

flies are buzzing round my head
vultures circling the dead
picking up every last crumb

digging deep into your pockets
baby birds squealing for attention
for chewed up morsels
rubbing their hands with glee

zigzagging around my brain
up my nose
in my eyes

diplomatic answers
to diplomatic questions
money for the generals

sending letter bombs
eating all the cookie crumbs

the big fish eat the little ones
the big fish eat the little ones
not my problem give me some

the faceless
please play along
you're only ever playing
don't wanna get your feet wet
stuck between commercials

**you can try the best you can try the best you can
the best you can is good enough
you can try the best you can try the best you can
the best you can is good enough**

this one isn't Jesus
this won't bring the missing back

this one gets the job done
the will of Allah
the word of God
preaching from the lecterns
tightening the stranglehold

why don't you stop beating yourself up?

**this one's optimistic
this one went to market
this one just came out of the swamp**

optimistic auto-suggestion
hello
hello
please play along
hymns numbered on a board
incarcerated punched and blown

just burnt spaghetti wires
call me back some other time
this song will not make you strong
this song will not give you brains

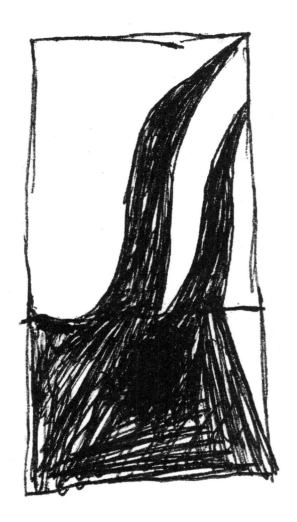

Trickle down compressor

make you look the other way
take the money and then run

this won't cure your loneliness
this won't bring back the disappeared
won't tell you what you need to know
won't give you brains
this won't get the job done
this won't get on TV
one pixel on a screen

this one drops a payload
fodder for the animals
living on animals farm

red ants black ants
no idea what we're doing
how could you be so naive?

this will not save you
not put the world to rights
will not solve you
will not fill the gap inside

honey from the honey bears
food is food and sex is sex

it's just not convenient
had my fill
want to defect

**you can try the best you can try the best you can
the best you can is good enough
you can try the best you can try the best you can
the best you can is good enough**

the optimist will drink and drive
the really nervous won't survive

optimistic foolish arseholes
tell you what you want to know
I am optimistic so fuck you all
you're not gonna get a rise out of me

when they were handing out the halos
I brought myself some old missiles

I built myself a bunker
I built myself an empire

**I'd really like to help you man
I'd really like to help you man
but I'm a nervous messed-up marionette floating
   round on a prison ship**

unless of course you're trying to hide
unless of course you're trying to hide
unless of course
you are trying to hide something

the names have changed the innocent

the innocent have been used to thicken
the soup
the soup can be used to feed the troops

I just can't seem to shake them off
they can smell bullshit a mile off
crawling in my trousers
crawling in my nose

how'd I ever get into this mess?
how can you be so utterly self obsessed?
when will you ever get out of bed?

you can try the best you can try the best you can
the best you can is good enough
you can try the best you can try the best you can
dinosaurs roaming the earth
dinosaurs roaming the earth
dinosaurs roaming the earth

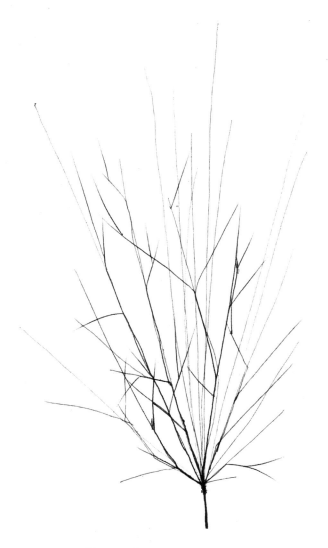

You were the one, you were the one

41 KID A

We've got heads on sticks

While you've got ventriloquists

Standing in the shadows at the end of my bed

The rats and children follow me out of town

COME ON KIDS![13]

---

13 everything is alive

all instruments
breathing has become . . . by proxy
breathing has . . . a delay on it
inanimate objects talk
time bends out of shape
edges distort and break off
a thin film of a different . . . volatile . . . rule of law . . . dimension
laws of nature changed

42 PYRAMID SONG

travelling around the earth in magnetic craft

landline motorways

I jumped into the river
black-eyed angels swam with me

a moon-full of stars and astral cars,
and all the figures I used to see

all my lovers were there with me
all my past and futures

and we all went to heaven in a little row boat
there was nothing to fear and nothing to doubt

43 DOLLARS & CENTS

there are better things
to talk about

be constructive
bear witness
we can use
be constructive
with yer blues

even when he turns the water blue
even when he turns the water green

don't get hung up
clutch at straws
form attachments
watch it go

we are cogs
sarky cogs
sqwirking round

why don't you quiet down?
why don't you quiet down?
why don't you quiet down?
why don't you quiet down?

(he wants a personality, American, free)
never stays

he never goes and he never stays
all over the neighborhood

maybe if I can see out here
maybe if I could see out of here
all over the clovers
oh let me out of here
all over all over all over all over

why don't you quiet down?
why don't you quiet down?
why don't you quiet down?
why don't you quiet down?*

*we are the DOLLARS & CENTS and the
   POUNDS and PENCE and the MARK and
   the YEN

we are going to crack your little souls

44 THE AMAZING SOUNDS OF ORGY

two-headed monsters
three-headed brides
nobody is free to do what they want
waited on hand and foot
the world's best-selling drug
comrades with mobile phones
the illegitimate sons
crawling out from under stones
daddy daddy I've come home

I want to see you smile again like diamonds in the
   dust
the amazing sound of the killing hordes
the day the banks collapsed on us

cease this endless chattering like everything is fine
when sorry is not good enough
sit in the back while no one drives

sing along here >
So glad so glad you're mine
So glad so glad you're mine

police on horseback
broken bones
we sit in the back while no one drives
a woman flutters her eyelashes in Washington
and bombs rain down in Sudan
women and children first
carry on smiling
and the world will smile with you

I'll laugh my nuts off the day the banks collapse
I'm all right jack
the day the banks collapse
the amazing sound of the killing hordes
human time bomb
we want to see them beg for life
chop off the fingers in the pie
I want to see you smile again
the day the banks collapse
the pure synthetic voice that says we're fine
limitless scenarios
limitless channels
on which to watch
who was right
and who was wrong

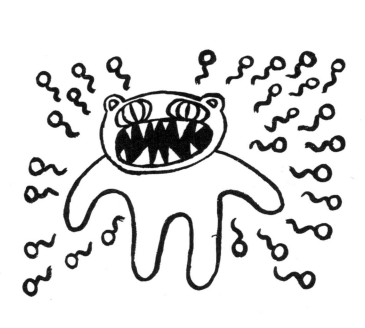

trussed up in tuxedos
we're the orchestra at the ball

when you're charity smiling
something's buried beneath the sidewalks

it will slide like slime through the walls
straw dogs to scare the crows

like the swish of electric doors
I don't get the point at all

I'm trying so hard to keep still
all the insides have been removed

these are bad clothes for rich people
this is the sound of boots crushing hands

in the end it was only a game
go back to the start again

and we'll pick you up by the heels
we'll shake it all out of you

too much time up in the air
not enough time on the floor

we slide like slime through your walls
we are cabbage patch gibbering dolls

we are straw dogs to scare the crows
you will not have heard this before

we're the orchestra at the ball
we beg for the scraps from your table

all we want is to be like you
we are very stupid people

it will slide like slime through the walls
it'll have all the insides removed

like the swish of electric doors
the attention of goldfish in bowls

I'm trying so hard to keep still
I don't get the point at all

these are bad clothes for rich people
patronised in magazines

drizzling sycophantic fawning
music to play to your clones

comforting sounds from the speakers
lying below their pillows

in the end it was only a game
go back to the start again

Optimistic auto-suggestion

I forgot why we started at all
these are bad clothes for rich people

and as every good editor knows
we are straw dogs to scare the straw crows

and after scant dinner
our lower ribs removed

when you're charity smiling
wining and dining

ballgowns and banquet speeches
feelin' cheated?

don't know what you mean

46 KINETIC

Toy soldiers marching to war
Clowns will do their tumbling

The sad claws of an old woman's hands
Helicopters circling

**You cannot stop the inevitable
You cannot stop the clockwork (turning)**

**You're being took for a ride
Pulling all the lazies**

**Please keep moving
Better keep moving**

**Don't fall asleep at the wheel
Can't you stop the children screaming?**

I waited for you but you never came

**Please keep moving
Better keep moving**

Kinetic Kinetic Kinetic Kinetic[14]

~ fee fi fo fum

---

14 Worrywort

no use dwelling in what might have been
water metal elliptical

when I'm in the dark
I forget the light
going in a circle
tell me I'm not dead
dead from the neck down
dead in the water
frozen in a pond
take hold of my hands
a-tissue-all-fall-down
tell that to my face
tell that to my face
crawling skeletons
no use telling them
what might have been
no excuses please
no apologies
to a walking skeleton

moving in the next world
don't find yourself in doldrums
too much to be done
no use dwelling on
no use dwelling on
what might have been
what might have been
this is not just a trap
this just stomach cramps
go up to the mike
go up to the mike
it's such a beautiful day
go and get some rays

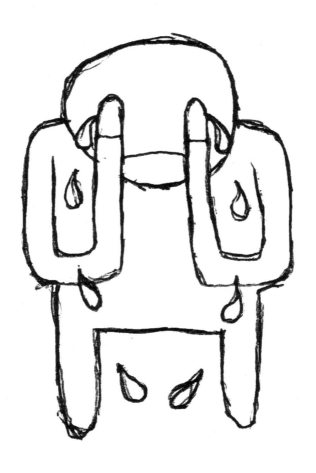

Today I just ran out of excuses

47 THE APPLICATION FORM

Icebergs sliding between desolate docks
Waterfalls of meltwater
Drumlins composed of bodies
You are not alone
You are observed
Gentle needles you can hardly feel

These woods and hills are the trademark of Woods
    and Hills PLC
Countryside developments
This stylised landscape is private intellectual
    property
Never lost
Always observed
Filthy glaciers floating in detritus-strewn tonic
    waters

With all this gone, everything I write
is a fucked approximation of my own furious,
misplaced and inaccurate nostalgia
The past never happened except in books

I have made these monsters
I have carved these glaciers from my frozen sperm
I coughed these icebergs

This dishwater, running fast past carcasses of the
    unfortunate
is what I pour down the sink,
an alchemical bilge of opportunity
Make-up, tears and vomit

It's not real
I can only touch these flooded waters,
like submerged grasses
Kick my heels in the silt

Catch me while you can,
because I am gone from here

Lumps become swellings
Wet swellings become poisoned weepings
Poisoned weepings become normal
All that's left are scars, scabs, wounds that won't
    heal

I regret to inform you that,
according to official criteria,
you are insufficiently miserable.
Therefore we are unable to help you.

If your circumstances should deteriorate please feel free to
    apply again.[15]

---

15 This is a Sketchbook

this is a sketchbook
open it at random
it's chopped up
recycled
scored out
it's a diary
it's a record

it's the sound of an echo chamber
the reflections in a hall of mirrors
if you don't have time for it then you are the same as me most
    of the time
we are goldfish in a bowl
the pages will come and go as we see fit
make what you will of it or ignore as you please
thank you for visiting

48 AMNESIAC

Someone hit me over the head
Now I'm the imposter
The real one's gone for ever
Blood all over the bathroom
Too much to drink

He didn't really cut it
Too much of a coward

You clown

49 TRANS-ATLANTIC DRAWL

I was tampered with
nipped and tucked for a magazine
smiling sweetly reclining in expensive desirable
    furniture
for your pleasure
in a magazine

in what the IN people are wearing now
in what clever people talk about
what you cannot afford
from a magazine

I was gone
now I'm back
with a new book
I wanna talk about
before we get to the ads

I guess I should know better but it keeps my weight
    down
look inside
nothing going on at all
the life you'd like to lead
white meat on a stick
if you wasn't just tryin' to make ends meet

you better start naming names

lifestyles of the rich and famous
help me please I am trapped

I am trapped in the society pages of a magazine
this is how it smells in first class
with a grin like road kill
with the bloody power of kings
fucking in the toilets of the Soho house
enough to wipe the president
I sneeze and it's an exocet
the flames are rising higher
I am tied to the stake

you better start naming names

**I was born
in a magazine
I am trapped in the society page
of your
magazine**

**do you see light at the end of the tunnel?
do you see light at the end of the tunnel?**

you better start naming names

do you see light at the end of the tunnel?
Jesus lord amen
yes I see light at the end of the tunnel
Jesus lord amen

*~ The Circus Is
Coming
Music
Lights
Cameras
Fog
Celebrity
Speakers
Electric Guitars
Drums
Synthesisers
Voices
Hearing
Damage*

50 BLACKMAIL PHOTO

Let me tell you your fortune

Dead by thirty-three

Bound

On your knees

With blackmail photos printed

In and out of rehab

You must have been a fuck-up

To even want this

Throw you a mirror in a million broken pieces

I'd like to know what you think of my book

We'd like to make a film of your life

~ We'd like to make a film of your life now that you are dead. Who can we contact? Who is executor of your estate?

51 IN LIMBO

Lundy, Fastnet, Irish Sea
I got a message I can't read

I'm on your side
Nowhere to hide
Trapdoors that open
I spiral down . . .

You are living in a fantasy world
You are living in a fantasy world

I'm lost at sea
Don't bother me
I've lost my way
I've lost my way

You are living in a fantasy world
You are living in a fantasy world
You are living in a fantasy world

The most beautiful woman in the world

Come back
Lundy, Fastnet, Irish Sea
Another message I can't read
Lundy, Fastnet, Irish Sea
Another message I can't read
Come back
Another message I can't read

Come back

~ woods where
no birds sing

52 THERE IS NO SUCH THING

There is no such thing as success

I had so much to say

And when I finally had a chance to say it

I stood there

Silently

Like a dumb motherfucker

53 THINGS FALLING APART

you try to run
you try to hide
things falling apart
there's no reason why

your cross is under your coat
things falling apart
but you don't give a shit

there's something right above
go up on the roof and pull it down
go on the roof and pick the boulders up

you turn to lie and I turned back
show me your hands

things falling apart
but it's not in my back yard

that is too simple
there is no plot

try to find a pattern
but there just isn't one

it's out of my sight
out of my control
things falling apart
no reason at all

say the words
nothing happens
make all the right moves
get all the right reactions

ten steps forward
fifteen steps back

things falling apart
they will not come back

leave me where you found me
no way out no way back
your cross is under your coat[16]

---

16 Pilgrims

Your grandparents welcome you with open arms
like they were just in the next room
a world where you can get a second chance
you can say you're sorry and be forgiven

The bloody power of kings

54 NOTHING

Nobody likes nothing
I certainly wish with all my heart that it did not exist

But wishing is not enough
We live in the real world where nothing does exist
We cannot just disinvent it

Nothing is not comprehensible
Neither you nor I have any hope of understanding just
    what it is and what it does

It is hard to know if nothing is actually nothing
And thus difficult to know if a policy of doing
    nothing is successful

Nothing
However effective it may have proved up to the present
Can hardly continue to do so indefinitely

If I had to choose
Between the continued possibility of nothing happening
And of doing nothing
I would unquestionably choose the latter

Or the former

55 ALL ETERNITY

caught like a human shadow at ground zero

cast in molten lava for all eternity in mid-action

halfway through telling someone it's over

putting out the cat

my skull through the window on impact

a row with your neighbour

their face looks familiar

frozen to the spot

as the flashbulbs erupt

then no chance of explanation

no defence against the witch hunt

~ apologies and condolences echoes that never die away

repeated in a lock through all eternity

all eternity

I'M NOT SCARED.

Please remember that past performance
is not necessarily a guide to future performance

a nice straight road with nothing coming
bowls is the sport for lazy folk like me
concorde comes to pick everybody up
a pyramid hovering over holland
nothing is not comprehensible
i crop zee big blocks hardcore
treefingered australopithecus
built in fashion obsolescence
fizzysticks (the final conflict)
oh dear how sad never mind
hotels and a swimming pool
dalek invasion with children
plunge to your fuckin doom
just the forest and the devil
please can i be your friend?
battlefield playground crop
do you see light at the end
optimistic auto suggestion
will you come back to me?
alps volcanoes snowstorm
snow evidence but on fire
electric golden handshake
sobbing mutant minotaur
branches into everything
on the run with the bears
cocaine disko all you like
doors that open and shut
bowlegged not listening
negative trees firedance
get out before saturday
bear interior decorator
designer outlet village
potential serial killer
a conflict of interests

deconstructed amnesiac
jonny zombie fckngscry
you sunk my battleship
crimean war wounded
theres no fighting here
you and whose army?
everything in its place
what might have been
facsimile transmission
enid blyton nightmare
hansons peacekeepers
no ideas im desperate
connect-the-dots bear
helicopterlandingpad
yet another minotaur
lots of sad minotaurs
lullaby in the bunker
target 80's landscape
red snow, bootprints
eaten & regurgitated
power failure report
people of today 2000
tumultous explosion
a bomb on the plane
i have born monster
glaciated landscape
this isnt happening
hotels and a glacier
cornwall big blocks
desolate blue scene
residential nemesis
please tick one box
a grin like roadkill
hotels, fire, glacier

unadorned minotaur
management buyout
underground house
mithras tauroctonos
land of freedom(tm)
my blue mindscape
giant wind machine
minos and a victim
burning black hole
volcanos bastardos
jungle shots on TV
bugsperm monster
exclamation marks
library scrawlings
room for easy golf
cloud cuckoo land
earthquake season
alternative advert
music for the rich
conspiracy theory
mountain triangle
swiss family bear
blue not listening
theater des todes
lost in the woods
advice for robots
dollars and cents
enjoyment ticket
business district
hissing like piss
carrots & sticks
things fall apart
citizen piranesi
a lethal cocktail

watch him skwirm
golden handshake
happy scarecrows
white wire demon
fragment horizon
how to disappear
how very twisted
wifey and hubbie
um like whatever
no blood no mess
photocopy okura
photocopy tower
wood of suicides
amnesiac london
insane_minotaur
marsh drowning
white mountains
googly minotaur
tearful minotaur
rescued piranesi
the easter bunny
revolving doors
offshore merger
amnesiac prison
perspective grid
detergent dream
happy accidents
hotel has fallen
realistic flames
beautiful story
nothing to fear
red sea eclipse
flying buttress
the best cliffs

bug sperm cave
red wire demon
ice age coming
acid minotaurs
amnesiac cryer
par permission
photocopy city
test specimens
trees & blocks
fantasy island
public private
rigid operator
teeth grinding
um like puffer
books all over
childrens bear
burning forest
indigos dream
popular music
insane_ukacid
citizen insane
lumpy terrain
scrappy cryer
except on fire
questionnaire
do not adjust
im not scared
devils crying
sitting ducks
is a nice day
lots of pools
celestial city
in the forest
devil in fire

swimming pool
zeetimebombs
walking bones
nervous again
wire minotaur
waste furnace
grand canyon
hypnosisbear
early mutant
ice drowning
encapsulated
drippy bears
mad junction
peacekeepers
morning bell
shamans tent
say the word
red minotaur
soot in snow
cornish acid
central park
burning city
single tower
inexplicable
lobster skin
persian city
stalking toy
the old face
test animals
trade center
trust no-one
angled trees
bears on air
selling fast

burning man
happyplants
shaky hands
bear growth
date stamps
kalashnikov
mongrel cat
despot bear
grim reaper
my attempt
in the maze
snow fields
powerlines
war village
bird blocks
right place
best hotels
target land
treefingers
terror bear
air cubana
bluespikes
ghost bear
knives out
dream list
jet projekt
ghost sign
optimistic
big blocks
polar bear
lightscape
care bears
teeth fuck
fast track

money bear
minos wall
two towers
wet advice
good news
hollywood
i backslash
open book
come back
nowadays
my phone
scarecrow
minotaur
idioteque
i am crap
trapped?
echo tree
backdrift
homeless
collision
integrity
a way in
das boot
astroboy
i am bad
roadmap
pyramid
diot son
in limbo
corridor
realistic
borealis
cut ups
acetate

immune
perform
twisted
success
fantasy
merger
a maze
london
gotcha
desert
pillars
clouds
adults
angels
poison
blocks
forest
sperm
clown
puffer
i wait
avert
kid a
amok
pogo
poet
pool
hole

Oh dear. How sad. Never mind

everything in its right place

everything
everything
everything
everything in its right place
in its right place
right place
right place

yesterday I woke up sucking a lemon

everything
everything
everything
everything in its right place
in its right place
right place
right place

there are two colours in my head

what is that you tried to say

tried to say . . .

kid A
we've got heads on sticks
while you've got ventriloquists

standing in the shadows at the end of my bed.

the rats & children follow me out of town . . .

come on kids

the national anthem

everyone
everyone around here
everyone is so near
is holding on.

everyone
everyone around here
everyone has got the fear
is holding on.

holding on.

how to disappear completely

that there
that's not me
I go
where I please
I walk through walls
I float down the liffey
I'm not here
this isn't happening
I'm not here
I'm not here.
in a little while I'll be gone
the moment's already past
yeah it's gone
and I'm not here

this isn't happening
I'm not here
I'm not here
strobe lights
and blowing speakers
fireworks
and hurricanes
I'm not here
this isn't happening
I'm not here
I'm not here.

treefingers

clink
clink
clink
optimistic

flies are buzzing round my head, vultures circling the dead,
    picking up every last crumb

the big fish eat the little ones, the big fish eat the little ones,
    not my problem give me some

you can try the best you can you can try the best you can, the
    best you can is good enough

this one's optimistic, this one went to market, this one just
    came out of the swamp

this one drops a payload, fodder for the animals, living on
    animal farm

you can try the best you can you can try the best you
can the best you can is good enough

I'd really like to help you man, I'd really like to help you
man

but I'm a nervous messed up marionette floating round
on a prison ship

you can try the best you can you can try the best you
can the best you can is good enough

you can try the best you can you can try the best

you can

dinosaurs roaming the earth

dinosaurs roaming the earth

dinosaurs roaming the earth

in limbo

(lundy fastnet irish sea I got a message I can't read)

I'm on your side

nowhere to hide

trap doors that open

I spiral down

(you are living in a fantasy world.)

I'm lost at sea

don't bother me

I've lost my way.

I've lost my way

(you are living in a fantasy world.)

(the most beautiful woman in the world.)

COME BACK!
COME BACK!
COME BACK!

(lundy fastnet irish sea I got a message I can't read)

idioteque

who's in the bunker? who's in the bunker?
women & children first and the children first and the children
I laugh until my head comes off
I swallow until i burst until i burst until I
who's in the bunker? who's in the bunker?
I have seen too much you haven't seen enough, you haven't
    seen enough, you haven't seen
I laugh until my head comes off
women and children first and children first and children
here I'm alive everything all of the time here I'm alive
    everything all of the time

ice age coming, ice age coming,
let me hear both sides, let me hear both sides, let me hear
    both
ice age coming, ice age coming
throw him on the fire, throw him on the fire, throw him on
we are not scaremongering
this is really happening
happening
we are not scaremongering
this is really happening
happening
mobiles chirping,
mobiles skwrking,
take the money run
take the money run
take the money
here I'm alive everything all of the time here I'm alive
    everything all of the time

morning bell

the morning
bell
the morning
bell
light another candle and release me, release me.
you
can keep
the furniture
bump
on
the
head

(howling down the chimney)
release me, release me
where did you park the car?
where did you park the car?
your clothes are on the lawn with the furniture
and I might as well
I might as well
sleepy jack
the fire drill
round and round and round and round and round and
round.
and round.

(everybody wants to know you
but nobody wants to be you
so you're walking walking walking walking walking
    walking walking walking walking walking walking
    walking walking walking walking walking)

motion picture soundtrack

red wine and sleeping pills help me get back to your
    arms
cheap sex and sad films help me get where i belong

I think you're crazy, maybe

stop sending letters, letters always get burnt
it's not like the movies, they fed us on little white lies

I think you're crazy, maybe

I will see you in the next life

And the lame shall walk
And the blind shall see
And that was last week